Oscar and the Blue Balloon

by Lily Rodgers

CLAY BRIDGES
PRESS

Oscar and the Blue Balloon

Copyright © 2022 by Lily Rodgers

Published by Clay Bridges Press in Houston, TX
www.ClayBridgesPress.com

All rights reserved. No part of this publication may be reproduced, stored in a retrieval system, or transmitted in any form by any means, electronic, mechanical, photocopy, recording, or otherwise, without the prior permission of the publisher, except as provided for by USA copyright law.

ISBN: 978-1-68488-025-6
ISBN: 978-1-68488-024-9
eISBN: 978-1-68488-023-2

Special Sales: Most Lucid Books titles are available in special quantity discounts. Custom imprinting or excerpting can also be done to fit special needs. Contact Lucid Books at Info@ClayBridgesPress.com

"To my family, whom I love very much"

All of a sudden,
Oscar was floating away from
his home and his family.

He was very sad and scared to leave,
but at the same time he was very
excited to see where he would go.

Oscar gently swayed
from side to side
while the balloon carried
him over the big blue ocean.

In the choppy waves, he saw amazing new
creatures that he had never seen before.

Colorful fish darted about in every which way
while a family of graceful sea turtles swam by.

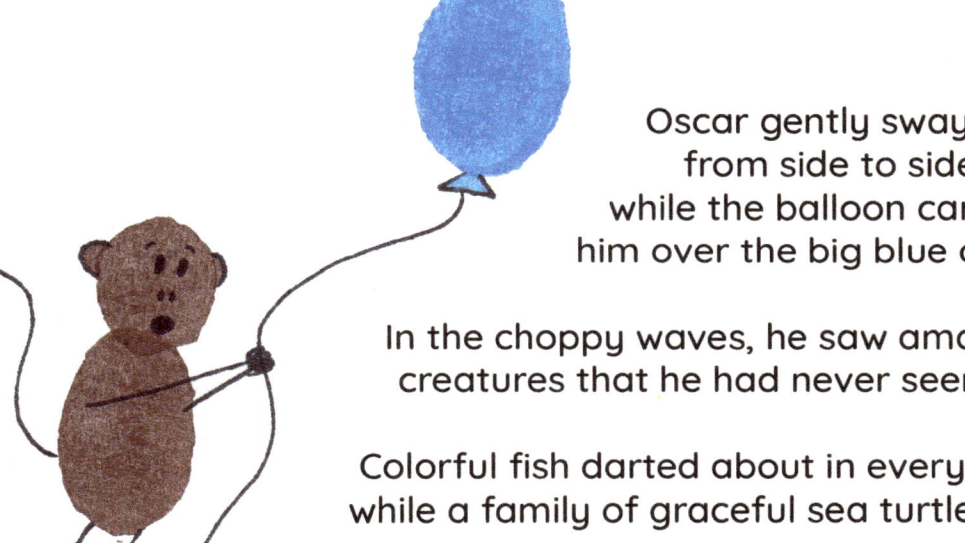

Oscar surprisingly saw land ahead of him.

As he was floating over this strange land, he noticed that nothing around him looked like his home in the jungle.

He saw trees, but the trees were colored differently. Reds, yellows, and oranges covered all the trees.

Oscar was confused because the trees in the jungle were always green.

Oscar heard a rustling in the bushes behind him.

When he turned around, there was a deer walking toward him with a smiling face that looked very friendly.

The deer said, "Hello, my name is Jett."

Oscar replied, "Hello, my name is Oscar."

After they were introduced to one another, Oscar began telling the story of how he had come to this strange land.

Then Oscar asked, "What is this place?"

Jett proudly declared that he had come to the Texas plains.

Since Oscar was in the Texas plains, he wondered what kinds of foods grew there, so he asked Jett.

Jett said, "Pecans, acorns, wheat, wild strawberries, wild chokecherries, onions, potatoes, and prickly pear cactus are the foods you will most likely find."

Then Oscar and Jett started to walk and talk about many different things.

After walking for a while, they ran into Autumn the rabbit, who was jumping in a pile of crunchy leaves.

Once Autumn saw the two friends, she joyfully hopped over to ask if they would like to jump in the leaves with her. Jett immediately agreed, and Oscar did too since he had never tried it before.

The trio had tons of fun for hours and hours. When the friends noticed how late it was getting, they decided to tell stories before going to bed.

While they watched the beautiful sunset dazzle the sky, the epic adventure of how Oscar had come to the plains was told.

That night there was a little raccoon in a tree very close to the three friends. He was just waking up from being asleep all day because he was a nocturnal animal.

The little raccoon came down the tree to chat with Oscar, Jett, and Autumn.

"Hi. My name is Rocky," he said. "I heard you telling stories to each other, and I thought maybe you would like to hear another."

The trio jumped up in excitement and quickly agreed. Rocky pulled out a book full of wonderful stories and told one to the sleepy friends.

When the story was finished, Oscar, Jett, and Autumn fell asleep knowing they had made a new friend.

As winter rolled in, Rocky told Oscar, Autumn, and Jett a different story from his book each evening before bed.

Every day the three friends played in the snow while Rocky slept. They made snow angels, built snowmen, and had snowball fights.

They loved eating the icicles that hung from the frost-covered trees.

The trio played all winter, with Rocky telling stories before bedtime, until it became spring.

Just after the last snowflake melted, spring arrived with its beautiful scent in the air.

Oscar, Jett, and Autumn were filled with awe and savored all the wonders of spring.

The trees grew fresh green leaves as flowers burst out of their buds to see the sunlight.

Bees and butterflies sipped the sweet nectar of colorful flowers while everything awakened from the long winter.

Animals emerged from their hiding places when they heard the sound of crisp, clear streams thawing as the sun warmed them.

Birds also filled the air with the delightful sound of chirping.

Now that spring had arrived and the winds had changed direction, Oscar became homesick.

The three friends had to think of a plan on how to get him back home to the jungle.

They all thought and thought very hard, but every idea seemed almost impossible.

Jett suggested that Oscar could fly on another balloon, but they didn't have one.

Autumn wondered if Oscar could make a hang glider out of leaves, but the leaves that grew around there weren't big enough.

All of a sudden,
a yellow kite came
s w o o s h i n g
through the air.

Oscar quickly climbed up
a tree and grabbed hold
of the kite string.

Then he brought it down
so the rest of his friends
could see it.

Oscar showed his friends the
yellow kite and said,
"This might be how I will get home,
but only if it is windy enough."

Jett excitedly replied,
"You are in luck!
It is almost always windy here."

So, on an especially windy day, Oscar said goodbye to all the new friends he had made.

With tears in his eyes, he left the Texas plains and started his journey back home to the jungle.

As he passed the ocean, the distinct smell of salt water tickled his nose. Brightly colored fish jumped out of the water, and the sea turtles waved as Oscar kept traveling.

After the ocean faded from view, he saw an amazing sight.

As the jungle trees began to surround him, he saw beautiful flowers and colorful birds everywhere. Oscar smelled the sweet air and knew that it had just rained. Everything sparkled as the sun hit the drops of rain on the pretty green leaves.

He was so very happy to be back home again.

Oscar sat on top of the forest canopy, and as he stared at the sunset he wondered if he would ever see his Texas friends again.

He thought of how Rocky would be starting to tell a new story. He wondered if Autumn missed him as much as he missed her. He remembered how Jett would have the answers to his many questions.

He just missed them all so much.

A moment later, Oscar heard some birds squawking. As he spun his head toward the commotion, Oscar was filled with delight because he saw that his family was not far away.

He swung from vine to vine until he was wrapped in his mother's arms.

With happy tears in her eyes, Oscar's mother held him tightly and asked him where he had been.

Oscar told his mother about his amazing journey, all he had learned, and the new friends that he had made.

He had had a wonderful adventure!

Even though he missed his new friends,
he was overjoyed to be home with his family!

Lily is the author and illustrator of *Oscar and the Blue Balloon*. She lives in Amarillo, Texas. She loves hanging out and playing games with her family. Lily and her family are fans of trying new things, especially new foods. She also enjoys hunting, fishing, reading, writing, and painting.

We want to say a special thank-you to our friends Chris and Tiffany for their expertise and the lovely picture of Lily.

Your kindness and generosity are amazing.
We are blessed to call you friends.

The Rodgers Family

CPSIA information can be obtained
at www.ICGtesting.com
Printed in the USA
LVHW071733110522
718480LV00009B/374